# A Dream Unfolds

## The Floral Art Society
## of Pakistan

# A Dream Unfolds

First published in 2008 for
**The Floral Art Society of Pakistan**
by Spirit of the Rose Publishing
71 Burford Road, Witney
Oxford OX28 6DR. UK


A catalogue record for this book is available
from the British Library
ISBN No 978-0-9543939-4-6


**VICE PRESIDENT- PUBLICATIONS**
Zareena Asghar Khan

**EDITOR**
Deborah Hutton

**PHOTOGRAPHY**
David Lloyd

**SCANNING, DESIGN AND PRODUCTION**
Annie Beagent - AB Imaging

**PRINTING**
Hill Shorter Limited

*A Dream Unfolds*

# *Foreword*

Nothing gives me more pleasure than to say "hello", through the medium of this book, to all my floral art friends in Pakistan.

The Floral Art Society of Pakistan – what rapid strides you have made since you formed officially in 1970, you were always way ahead; I remember a number of your members, including your President, courageously coming to England to compete at the National Show of the National Association of Flower Arrangement Societies AND winning many prizes.

No matter what the style, Pakistan is always new.

The flowers cannot speak for themselves but they can, in the hands of talented flower arrangers, strike a happy note among all those who see them, and the more you look at flowers the more you have to ask yourself "where have they come from?"

They are not manufactured by any one person or one country; they come from a seed, just like us, and the more you look at them the more you realise that they set us human beings such a fine example. Although some are tall and some are short, some are bold others are shy, they do not seem to vie with each other for supremacy, nor do they show any jealousies as far as we know, they just seem to give love and beauty to all who see them, and that is the work of this Society; to spread love and beauty – just like the flowers.

**JULIA CLEMENTS, OBE, VMH**
**Life Vice-President NAFAS**

# Introduction

The Floral Art Society of Pakistan (FASP) has great pleasure in presenting *A Dream Unfolds*: a book which commemorates the enchantment that floral art brings in to our lives. The book also celebrates Pakistan's three year tenure of WAFA 2005 – 2008 and the 9th World Flower Show.

The designs in this book were inspired by a five thousand year history, extraordinary landscapes, a kaleidoscope of flora and fauna and a fusion of cultures from across the world. The artists were able to fuse a rich variety of local plant material with futuristic designs and traditional training to produce masterpieces of joy.

The contents of *A Dream Unfolds* were compiled by the members of FASP. The rich visual imagery reflecting the spirit of Pakistan was captured by David Lloyd. It acknowledges the talent and skills of the gifted designers, and infinite palette of flowers, fruits and plant material in extraordinary settings across the country.

I observed David closely during the photo-shoots. His love for flowers and eye for detail was evident in every photograph that he took. The brilliant photographs in this book are a testament to the expertise of the designers and the near genius of the capturer.

We are thankful to everyone who helped us create a bold statement of the joyful world of floral art. Without their support, we would not have been able to share our hopes and dreams expressed in the language of flowers with the floral art community and friends throughout the world. We hope that this book will help promote the art of flower arranging, and cultural exchange between nations.

**Shahimah Sayeed**
**President**
**World Association of Flower Arrangers 2005-2008**

# *Acknowledgements*

It was a privilege and a pleasure to produce a book on the rich floral culture of Pakistan on the occasion of the 9th World Flower Show.

Photographer David Lloyd needs no introduction. His artistry and skill, evident through his photography, left us spellbound. Even the most mundane of items looked superb – "who said the camera never lies?"

Deborah Hutton's help, hard work and guidance were invaluable. We could not have achieved this without her.

Both these lovely people put up with the hot sun, soothed the harassed committee and showed patience with all our club members and personnel staff.

My thanks go to the Presidents of the three main chapters of the Floral art Society of Pakistan in Karachi, Lahore and Islamabad for their suggestions and ideas, and for organizing and supporting the photographic shoots. Finally, my thanks go to all the people who created the beautiful arrangements for the book.

This book would not have been possible without true friends who lent their homes or obtained permissions for the use of special venues as backgrounds.

I hope this book will give you a glimpse of Pakistan's natural beauty, culture and diversity in flora and fauna: we wish that you have as much pleasure going through it as we had in making it.

**Zareena Asghar Khan**
**Vice President - Publications**

The venues used for the photographic shoots included the private residences and gardens of the following:- Zareena and Ghulam Asghar Khan, Azra and Younas Khan, Khurshid and Ebrahim Hasham, Farida and M. Kalim, Shahimah and Ashraf Sayeed, Marrokh and Vice Admiral Ahmad Hayat (Chairman, KPT), Mohatta Palace Museum gardens, Beach Hut of Mrs. Nafisa Tapal at French Beach in Karachi.
Residence of Mrs. Ambreen Irfan and Noor Gardens in Lahore.
Serena Hotel, Shahzad Farm, Daman-e-Koh and Pir Sahawa in Islamabad.

23

34

*Index*

**Basant (Kite Festival)**
**Zarin Patel**
page 1
Areca palm
Sansevieria trifasciata
Meremia tuberose
(wood rose vine)
Cassia fistula seed pods

**Cycles**
**Farida Kalim**
page 2
Delonix regia beans
Kalanchoe beharensis
Black fungas
Phoenix dactylifera husk

**A Dream Unfolds**
**Ruhina Khalid**
page 5
Phoenix dactylifera
Lilium

**Colours of the Deep**
**Zareena Asghar Khan**
page 6
Brassica oleracea sabellica
Stargazer lily
Gladiolus
Senecio cruentus
Gypsophila
Tillandsia
Chrysanthemum

**Rhythmic Roots**
**Sayeeda Salahjec**
page 9
Lilium
Coco spathes
Buddha seed pods
Philodendron

**Evolution**
**Farida Kalim**
page 10
Bauhinia sp.
Caryota mitis seed strand
Kalanchoe beharensis
'Bronze Velvet'

**On a Quiet Beach**
**Salma Ansari**
pages 12 and 13
Driftwood
Laminaria sp. (Kelp)
Straw spheres
Senecio cruentus
Codiaeum croton

**Phantom of the Opera**
**Oofi Khan**
page 14
Cocos spathes
Moss
Helianthus
Vine

**Oriental Strains**
**Talat Hashimi**
page 15
Cocos spathe
Caryota mitis
Roystonea regia
Jasminium humile
Roses of Attar
Henna painting

**Bed of Floral Delights**
**Asma Ansari**
page 16
Iris xipium (hybrids)
Chrysanthemum
Gladiolus
Gypsophila
Aspidistra eliator
Epipremnum aureum
Danae racemosa

**Papillon Gladioli**
**Yasmin Sohail**
page 17
Cocos fibre
Livistona rotundifolia
Gladiolus

**Elegance**
**Naila Abras**
page 18
Iris xiphium
(hybrids)
Aspidistra
 eliator
Draceana

**Basket of Delight**
**Aisha Zahid**
page 18
Bringals (sic.)
Citrus limon
Cineraria
Freesia, Iris
Brassica oleracea
gemmifera
Zingiber officinale

**Cineraria and**
**Plaited Palm**
**Farhana Azim**
page 18
Senecio cruentus
Sabal palmetto

**A Ray of Hope**
**Tanvir Khwaja**
page 19
Sansevieria trifasciata
Philodendron
Schefflera arboricola
Alocassia
Canna indica variegata
Rumohra adiantisformis
Banyan root
Tillandsia usenoides

**Beauty Resting**
**Dilshad Irani**
page 20
Stargazer lilies
Dendrobium orchids
Draceana reflexa
Monstera delicosia

**Aftaba (Moghul samovar)**
**Wiqarunnisa Bolani**
page 20
Lilium 'La Reve'
Gladiolus
Draceana

**Designed by Nature**
**Shahla Khan**
page 20
Banyan tree roots
Lilium
Phalces
Cassia fistula seed pods

**After Hogarth**
**Nabila Khawaja**
page 21
Aspidistra eliator
Anthurium andreanum
Lilium Stargazer
Spathiphyllum wallisii
Spathodea campanulata
 seed pods

**Nature's Bounty**
**Asma Ansari**
page 22
Epipremnum aureum
Draceana
Aspidistra eliator
Cactus
Dianthus caryophyllus
Antirrhinum majus
Cobea scandens
Cyperus alternifolius
Salix babylonica
Salix caprea

**Contrasts**
**Saida Shahabuddin**
page 23
Lilium hemerocallis
 festalis
Fescue
Asparagus officinalis
Cocos nucifera
Gypsophila
Terminalia catappa
Leucaena leucacephala

**Noor Jehan**
**Ambreen Irfan**
page 24
Saccharin munja
Gerbera
Dianthus caryophyllus
Salix babylonica
Echinops
Corchorus olitorius

**Fun with Geometry**
**Oofi Khan**
page 25
Euphorbia milii
Agave sisalina
Vine
Spathodea campanulata

**On the Rocks**
**Zarin Patel**
page 26
Bannesteria vine (sphere)
Roystonea regia spathe
Cocos coir
Cocos spathe
Euphorbia milii var.
 tulearensis

91

**Snake Charmer**
**Nafisa Tapal**
**page 26**
Erythrina variegate
Cactus
Palm flower
Vine

**On the Waters Edge**
**Shahimah Sayeed**
**page 27**
Driftwood
Dendrobium
Philodendron foliage

**Step Through The Window**
**Shahimah Sayeed**
**page 28**
Driftwood
Phalaenopsis
Philodendron
Spathodea campanulata

**Sunset over the Arabian Sea**
**Zareena Asghar Khan**
**page 29**
Gerbera
Gladiolus
Chrysanthemum
Ficus elastica variegata

**Capture the Moment**
**Shahimah Sayeed**
**page 29**
Mangrove wood
Phoenix dactylifera husk
Strelitzia reginae

**Colours of Henna**
**Aisha Zahid**
**page 30**
Sanseviera trifasciata
Gladiolus
Capiscum frutescena
Rosa sp.
Freesia
Capsicum annuum
Punica granatum
Brassica oleracea gemmifera
Fragaria
Citrus limon

**Parsi Ceremonial Doorway**
**Zarin Patel**
**page 31**
Garlands of Roses of Attar
Calendula officinalis
Tagetes

**Henna Festival**
**Shanaz Azher Mahmoud**
**page 32**
Rosa sp.
Prunus dulcis (almond)
Helichrysum
Oryza sativa + crocus sativus
Capsicum frutescens
Sinapsis alba oil

**Wedding Table**
**Naveen Nooruddin**
**page 32**
Rose of Attar
Calendula officinalis
Senecio cruentus
Duranta repens
Ranunculus
Phoenix dactylifera seeds

**Truck Art**
**Yasmin Sohail**
**page 33**
Livistona rotundifolia
Serenoa repens
Crassula ovata
Schefflera arboricola
Jasminium indica

**Snake Dance**
**Dr. Shahida Anwer**
**page 34**
Hetrophragma adenophylum pods
Monstera deliciosa
Tagetes

**Ancient and Modern**
**Safia Munawar**
**page 34**
Aspidistra eliator variegata
Dracaena reflexa 'Song of India'
Monstera deliciosa
Chrysanthemum
Liana vine

**Symphony of Spring**
**Farhana Azim**
**page 35**
Chrysanthemum
Gladiolus
Rosa sp.
Danae racemosa
Draceana
Citrus reticulata ornate

**Oriental Splendour**
**Talat Hashimi**
**page 36**
Calendula officinalis
Tagetes cultivars
Citrus limon
Flower of Musa sapientum
Aubergine
Dhupatta (shawl) from Swat Valley
Chair from Thar

**In the Style of the Moghul Period**
**Shahimah Sayeed**
**page 37**
Lilium
Dianthus caryophyllus
Rosa sp.
Asparagus meyerii
Cortaderia
Fern

**The Enchanting East**
**Ruhi Sayid**
**page 38**
Rosa sp.
Jasminium sambac

**Entwined**
**Batul Haji**
**page 39**
Fruit of Caryota sp.
Anthurium andreanum
Kalanchoe beharensis

**Antique Samovar**
**Samina Shahid Rafi**
**page 40**
Gladiolus
Rosa sp.
Chrysanthemum
Calendula officinalis
Jasminum indica garland
Brassica oleracea

**Antiquity**
**Neveen Syed**
**page 40**
Garlands of Roses of Attar
Bellis (white flower garlands)

**Sculptured Beauty**
**Nargis Jaffer**
**page 41**
Gladioli
Ficus elastica
Bringals (sic)
Magnolia acuminate
Eucalyptus bark

**Worlds Apart**
**Neveen Syed**
**page 42**
Aloe vera
Yucca aloifolia
Amaryllis belladonna
Dried gourds

**More Jazz**
**Samina Salm**
**page 42**
Anthurium andreana
Ficus elastica 'Black Queen'
Rosa sp.
Zea mays

**Delight in Bright Colours**
**Razia Reza**
**page 42**
Sansevieria trifasciata
Anthurium andreanum
Chrysanthemum
Dianthus caryophyllus
Pine cone
Cane

**Hope**
Farida Hassan
page 43
Amaryllis belladonna
Allium sp.
Callistemon
Salix
Hyophorbe lagenicaulis
spathe
Caryota seeds
Maranta sp.

**Nature's Beauty**
Samina Alvi
page 44
Bamboo
Anthurium andreanum
flowers and foilage
Liana vine

**Nature into Art**
Asma Haroon
page 45
Salix spheres and rings
Vitis
Chrysanthemum
Gerbera

**Good Luck Charm**
Anjum Rehman
page 46
Caryota mitis
Pandanus variegatus
Gladiolus

**Vertically Challenged**
Erum Kamram
page 47
Dendrobium orchids
Cane

**On Parade**
Samina Salman
page 47
Salix, woven
Dendrobium orchid

**Palm Spathe with Lillies**
Amenah Raheel
page 48
Chlorophytum comosum
Aloe Vera
Lilium
Iris xiphium (hybrids)

**Deja vu**
Ambreen Irfan
page 49
Lilium Lancefolium
Livistona rotundifolia
Palamusa fern

**Angles**
Musarrat Zain
page 50
Dianthus caryophyllus
Cyperus alternifolius

**Sound of Rolling Stone**
Saima Musarrat
page 50
Pandanus variegatus

**Blooming Ash**
Nishat Kazmi
page 50
Monstera deliciosa
Fraxinas nigra
Casablanca lily

**Between the Lines**
Ambreen Irfan
page 51
Saccharum Munja
Corylus avellana
'Contorta'
Lilium

**The Dancer**
Khadija Jamal
page 42
Pritchardia pacifica
Latania Lontaroides
Frangipanni foilage
Rosa sp.
Dianthus caryophyllus

**Mountain Air**
Talat Hashimi
page 53
Sansevieria trifasciata
Gypsophila
Wild grasses
Cacti
Succulents

**Flowering of a Dream**
Farida Kalim
page 54
Agave Pelmeri
Phalaenopsis
Meremia tuberosa vine

**Neptune's Garden**
Farida Kalim
page 55
Agave pelmeri
Phalaenopsis orchid
Tillandsia
Sea fan

**Penninsula**
Wiqarunnisa Boolani
page 56
Ruscus hypoglossum
Gladiolus
Bamboo sheath
Tillandsia usneoides

**Flight of Fantasy**
Yasmin Sohail
page 57
Phoenix dactylifera
Strelitzia reginea
Sabal palmetto
Alpinia calcarata

**Shalimar**
Zeeni Afrida
page 58
Chrysanthemum
Rosa sp.
Eriobotrya japonica
Iris xiphium

**Ascent**
Farhat Zaman
page 59
Aloe vera
Iris xiphium (hybrids)
Eriobotrya japonica
Citrus aurantium
Citrus limon
Vine, bleached
Alpinia calcarata
variegate

**Ode to Autumn**
Anjum Muddassir
page 60
Magnolia grandifolia
Helianthus
Areca palm stem
Phoenix dactylifera

**Perfect Partners**
Oofi Khan
page 61
Zamia palm
Strelitzia reginea
Tillandsia usneoides
Mintola (sic)

**Splash of Green**
Salma Moshin
page 61
Areca palm seed head
Cocos spathes
Duranta erecta
Reindeer moss
Dried contorted palm
leaves
Driftwood

**Levels of Delight**
Nasreen Amjad
page 61
Cocos spathes
Asparagus meyerii
Ficus elastica variegata
Cyperus alternifolius
Draceana, Capsicum
Gourd
Brassica olearacea botrytis
Citrus reticulate deliciosus
Gladiolus
Calendula officinalis

93

**Up Up and Away**
**Ghazala Rafique**
**page 62**
Baucarnia
Agave sisalina
Salix
Sansevieria

**Inspired by Multan pottery**
**Shahimah Sayeed**
**page 63**
Gladiolus
Tulipa sp.
Iris xiphium (hybrids)
Limonium sinuatum
Dianthus caryophyllus

**Necklace and Earings**
**Yasmin Saleh**
**page 64**
Hyophorbe lagenicaulis, dried
Arucaria
Various palm seeds and pulses
Dried flowers

**Necklace and Earings**
**Raana Shahmim Zafar**
**page 64**
Various seeds
 including triticum
Vitis
Sea fan coral

**Traditional Hand Painting**
**Page 64**

**Necklace and Earings**
**Saima Musarrat**
**page 65**
Casuarina equisetifolia
seeds
Kabli (sic) seeds
Inga dulcis
 (pithecolobium dulce)
Parridge (sic) seeds

**Dance of Colours**
**Rukhsana Ali**
**page 66**
Gladiolus
Chrysanthemum
Ranunculus
Aspidistra eliator
Iris xiphium (hybrids)
Cassia fistula sed pod
Statice limonium

**Vertical Support**
**Khadija Jamal**
**page 66**
Pritchardia pacifica
Aspidistra eliator
Areca Triandra (woven)
Dianthus caryophyllus
Gerbera
Anthurium andraenum

**Whispering Winds**
**Ruhi Sayid**
**page 67**
Gerbera
Phoenix dactylifera
seeds

**Fresh Moment**
**Zarin Patel**
**page 68**
Roystonea regia spathe
Lotus seed pods
Cocos nuciferas nuts
Salix babylonica
Pekinensis 'Tortuosa'
Anthurium andreanum
Aspidistra eliator

**Calligraphy 'Allah'**
**Zainab Mohammed**
**page 68**
Cocos spathes
Agave
Brassica oleracea sabel-
lica
Fungus
Strelitzia foilage

**Timeless**
**Farida Khawar**
**page 68**
Area palm spathes
Fungus
Gilia californica
(prickly pear)
Banyan tree root
Aloe vera
Succulents
Tillandsia usneoides
Fasciated branch

**Evolution**
**Naushaba Khalil**
**page 69**
Salix babylonica
Salix spheres
Lens culinaris spheres
Cane spheres
Aspidistra eliator
Aloe vera root

**Rustic Splendour**
**Oofi Khan**
**page 70**
Heliconia
Anthurium andreatum
Buddha seed pods

**Outline**
**Yasmin Saleh**
**page 70**
Ixora
Ficus elastica
Banyan root
Chrysanthemum
Citrus limon
Dracaena bloom

**Escape**
**Ambreen Irfan**
**page 70**
Saccharum
 Spontaneum
Gerbera

**Other Side of Midnight**
**Ambreen Irfan**
**page 71**
Cocos husk
Rosmarinus officinalis
Capsicum

**Snake Charmer's Delight**
**Shauket Ashfaque**
**page 71**
Capsicum frutescens
Sansevieria trifasciata
Cassia fistula seed pods

**Meeting Place**
**Samini Salman**
**page 72**
Triticum
Blooms of the
Sumbal Tree
Oryza sativa

**Decorative Art**
**Anjum Rehman**
**page 73**
Phoenix dactylifera spathes
Cassia fistula seed pods
Bamboo slices
Inga Dulcis
(Pithecolobium dulce)

**Duet**
**Qudsia Akbar**
**page 73**
Ficus elastica
Rosa sp.
Xerophyllum tenax
 (Bear Grass)

**Ship Ahoy!**
**Zarin Patel**
**page 74**
Cocos spathes
Areca palm
Fresh Acacia seed pods
Spathodea campanulata
Delonix regia seed pods
Codiaeum croton

**Combinations**
**Shahla Khan**
**page 75**
Philodendron
Phoenix dactylifera
Lillium
Kaffir lily foilage
Pandanus variegatus

**A Natural Corner**
**Qurratulain Aamir**
**page 76**
Calotropis procera
'Hamilton'

**Swirls of Nature**
**Nasreen Khalid Anwer**
**page 77**
Anthurium andreanum
Chrysanthemum
Alocasia metallica
Hapene (Skeletonised
phormium tenax)
Bauhinia sp.

**Elegance**
**Qudsia Akbar**
**page 78**
Areca palm
Anthurium andeanum

**Escape**
**Ghazala Rafique**
**page 78**
Hedera stems
Salix
Draceana sanderiana
Helianthus

**Peacock Plate**
**Wiqarunnisa Boolani**
**page 79**
Gladiolus
Ranunculus
Chrysanthemum
Areca Palm
Duranta
Calendula officinalis
Citrus ichangense variegate
Linaria purpurea
Cobaea scandens

**Ray of Hope**
**Anjum Muddaser**
**page 80**
Phoenix dactylifera
Ficus elastica
Draecena
Clerodendron bealei

**Gift of Nature**
**Yasmin Raziuddin**
**page 80**
Citrus aurantium
Salix babylonica with
moss
Hyophorbe lagonicaulis
spathes

**Gossiping Gourds**
**Ambreen Irfan**
**page 80**
Gerbera
Gourds
Phoenix dactylifera

**Caged**
**Riffat Chugtai**
**page 81**
Anthurium andreanum
Heliconia
Strelitzia reginae
Aspidistra eliator
Beaucarnia recurvata

**Spirals at Play**
**Aisha Tariq**
**page 82**
Ficus elastica
Dianthus
caryophyllus
Stripped cane

**Contrast in Texture**
**Naushaba Khalil**
**page 82**
Dried cacti
Cordyline Red edge
Philodendron lime
Phoenix dactylifera

**Weaving threads of**
**Beauty**
**Samia Sikander**
**page 82**
Salix stems
Gerbera

**Swirls and Curls**
**Ruhina Khalid**
**page 82**
Ficus elastica
Phoenix dactylifera
Gerbera

**Shapes and Shadows**
**Ghazala Abdullah**
**page 83**
Aspidistra eliator variegata
Cassia fistula seed pods
Ricinus communis seed
head

**Gift of Nature**
**Musarrat Zain**
**page 84**
Aspidistra eliator
Philodendron
Jacaranda procera seed
pods
Palm seeds

**From the Deserts of Sind.**
**Talat Hashimi**
**page 84**
Driftwood
Cocos nuciferas
Aloe vera
Cacti
Various succulents

**Ancient and Modern**
**Ghazala Abdullah**
**page 85**
Anthurium andraenum
Chrysanthemum
Cocos pods
Philodendron
Fungus

**Flowers with Antiquity**
**Farhana Azim**
**page 86**
Delonix regia (Flame of
the Forest)
Agave filifera variegata
Tectona grandis

**Snake Charmer**
**Ambreen Irfan**
**page 86**
Laminaria sp.
Rosa sp.

**Sculptured Beauty**
**Yasmin Sohail**
**page 87**
Laminaria sp. (kelp)
Betula bark
Dried cactus
Dianthus caryophyllus

**Ballerina**
**Shameeli Iftikhar**
**page 88**
Aspidistra eliator
Corypha umbraculifera
Cocos spathes
Dianthus caryophyllus

**Calligraphy**
**Qudsia Akbar**
**page 88**
Cocos spathes
Rosa sp.
Meremia tuberose
(wood rose)
Fungus
Herbs
Philodendron

**Eastern Hospitality**
**Ambreen Irfan**
**page 88**
Rosa sp.
Areca catechu
Thuya orientalis

**Rhapsody in Silver**
**Sayeeda Salehjee**
**page 89**
Cocos spathes
Dried palm spathes
Seed pod selection

**Rhotas Fort**
**Shahimah Sayeed**
**page 90**
Rosa sp.
Alcea rosea
Callistemon
Papaver somniferum
Lathyrus odoratus
Tulipa sp. (Field lily)

**Driftwood Enhanced**
**with Foliage**
**Shahimah Sayeed**
**page 96**
Asparagus meyerii
Chaemerops humilis
Philodendron
Salix babylonica spheres
Canna indica